Tigers & Other Lilies

HOWARD MOSS

Tigers &

Other Lilies

Drawings by Frederick Henry Belli

Atheneum   *New York*   *1977*

"Catnip and Dogwood," "Clammy Campion," "Cowslip," "Harebell," "Horse Chestnut Tree," "Ostrich Fern," and "Viper's Bugloss, Wolfberry, Red Hot Cattail, Spiderwort" originally appeared in *The New Yorker*.

Library of Congress Cataloging in Publication Data

    Moss, Howard, 1922
       Tigers and other lilies.
       SUMMARY: Brief humorous poems inspired by plants with animals in their names.
       1. Plants—Juvenile poetry. 2. Humorous poetry, American. [1. Plants—Poetry. 2. Humorous poetry. 3. American poetry] I. Belli, Frederick. II. Title.
    PZ8.3.M845Ti   77–1998
    ISBN 0–689–30592–3

For my nephew, David Evans

Contents

Tigers & Other Lilies

Introductory Poem

Though only God
Can make a tree,
I find it odd
That so many

Are named for in-
sects, beasts, and birds,
And make such in-
teresting words.

The same is true
Of plants and flowers
In this zoo
Of beastly bowers.

Pussy Willow

"Whose pussy willow
   Are you?" said a pussy
   Willow to another
   Pussy willow who
   Stood not far away
   Giving the time of day
   To the first pussy willow.
"Your buds of fur
   Are the ones I prefer,"
   Said the first
   In a burst
   Of ardor.

   Said Two,
"If only
   Buds could purr,
   They'd murmur,
   'Our response
   Must be—
   For the nonce—
   Equivocal . . .
   You see,
   We're rather
   Emotionally involved
   With an oak, an alder,
   An aspen, and a quince.' "

Snapdragon

"That loud-mouthed animal! I can't imagine
  Why *I'd* be named for *him*," said the snapdragon.

"Those hot, dry scales! That snort! That evil
  Reptilian look! It beats the devil

  How such an ugly monster out of myth
  And *I* could be mentioned in the same breath!"

  The dragon, opening his mouth to reply,
  Nervously twitched his tail, and blinked.
  "I *say* . . . that's a bit . . . I mean . . . What a *lie*! . . ."
  But before he could finish, he became extinct.

Horse Chestnut Tree

Though you may find chestnuts
At the grocery,
It's ten to one
That you'll never see
Horse chestnut trees
At the A & P.

It's getting harder
To see horses, too—
There's no lack
At the track,
But too few
At the zoo.

Leopard Flower

Said a leopard, "My goodness! What's
Going on? The leopard flower's dots
Look like the burns
Of cigarette butts
Or a person covered with spots!"

Viper's Bugloss, Wolfberry, Red Hot Cattail, Spiderwort—

There are some plants
I'd hate to see
Like the Viper's Bugloss
And the Wolfberry.

It would make me ill
Just to come up short
On the Red Hot Cattail
Or the Spiderwort.

Crab Grass

What's lump, half shell, or whole?
No, no, not filets of sole!
Guess again. No, cod's too drab.
You've got it. It's a crab!

What makes crab grass a mess?
The mess it makes of a terrace,
A garden, yard, or lawn,
By thrusting in between
Gravel, brick,
Stone, or rock
Unwelcome claws of green.

Kangaroo Vine

A kangaroo vine
Has been known to twine
Up anything crooked
Or serpentine.
It can also go
Vertically up—
Rising erratically
Quite acrobatically—
Or, should it want to be
Flat, horizontally.

After it crouches,
A kangaroo maybe
Will stand up and show you
A kangaroo baby—
Which kangaroos hide,
By the way, in their pouches.

Pignut

The pignut is a nut
Pigs find delicious,
Especially when the shell's
Already cracked.

Pigs never, never, *never*
Wash the dishes—
Or anything else,
As a matter of fact.

Ostrich Fern

What likes to thrust its head in the sand,
And stands—but never takes a stand—
The picture of neutrality
Escaping from reality,

Withdrawn to a degree,
The ostrich—is it he?

An ostrich *fern*? It's like an ostrich. Sort of.
Two legs, though, it doesn't have the support of.

Skunkbrush

The smell of skunk
Is like old junk.

The skunkbrush, too,
Smells kind of punk.

Shrimp Plant

A shrimp plant's unlike a shrimp because
It isn't better with cocktail sauce.

Wormwood

Is a worm
A big germ
Or a little snake?
I can't figure it out,
For heaven's sake!

Is wormwood good?
Or bad? Or so-so?
If offered some,
Would you say,
"I sup*pose* so?"

If offered none,
Would you say, "Oh, *please*!
They're my very,
Very
Favorite trees?"

Maybe it's a kind
Of wine or berry?
Or a buttercup?
Or a sour cherry?
I've just looked it up:

It's a bitter herb,
According to Webster's
International Third
Diction-
ary.

Bearberry

Bearberry is a plant
Bears like to nibble.
I think we'd find its taste
Quite terrible.

I wonder why bears
Like to eat bearberry?
It sounds quite odd to me.
Mighty! VERY!

Ox-Eye Daisy

Than an ox
An ox-eye
Daisy's
Dumber,

But it grows
Like crazy
Every
Summer.

Clammy Campion

The clam is clammy
From Maine to Miami,
And hunted with zest
Even further west:
It's the native gismo
At a place called Pismo
Beach, where you gnaw
Clams cooked, clams raw;
They're served with a touch of—
And sometimes too much of—
The hottest Tabasco
In Tijuana or Taxco.

Though the clammy campion
Is damper and clammier
Than the *un*clammy campion,
And much more campier,
Of all of the campia
It's considered the champion.

Cowslip

Corpulent and calm, cows chew their cud.
In March, they march around in mire and mud.
They munch and march around and munch some more,
Drink punch, then brunch, have luncheon, or
For dinner, as a change of menu,
They chew and march and munch, and when you
Milk them, why, they go on eating,
Quite unaware that they're repeating
Exactly what they did before,
Which is to march and munch some more.

Those with a legal education,
Cry, after years of rumination,
"Clear the court! A change of venue!"
Then relapse with a kind of genu-
flection while they take their fill
Of sweet-breath-making chlorophyll.
After the grass has led to greed,
A few of them lie down and read
"The Sensuous Cow" by Sitting Bull.
—They need far less Sen-Sen than you.

The cowslip, on the other hand,
Is a marsh marigold, or/and
A primrose. And *some* say, and/or
A bore.

Dandelion

The dandelion's gold, but soon grows gray,
Then goes to seed and blows away.

One New York lioness in furs
Writes letters to the press: "Dear Sirs,
Although I'd be the last to boast—
What becomes a legend most?"

Harebell

Hares are rabbits
Who live in lairs
And have hare habits
And rabbit hairs.

If you give the harebell
A little swing,
And you listen closely,
It goes ting-a-ling.

Larkspur

When someone staring at a Jackson Pollack,
Says, "What a lark! It's so symbolic!"
You don't have to bother looking up the word:
He means a frolic
Not a singing bird.

To keep confusion to a minimum,
Flowers—each and every one of them—
Have both a Latin and a common name:
Larkspur and *delphinium*
Are the same.

Toadstool

A toad won't sit on a stool,
That is, it won't as a rule,
Or a couch, or a chair,
Or the floor, or a stair,
Or a donkey, a horse, or a mule.

It likes to sit in a pond,
Look up and down and around,
Then hop to the grass,
Or a muddy morass,
And squat there for days on end.

On the *other* hand,

A toadstool is a mushroom, more than filling.
If it has the last laugh, you'll find it killing.

31

Horse Radish

Horses have a reason for putting on airs:
They wear horseshoes, and they wear two pairs.

Horse radish is a spice that tastes so hot
You break out in a sweat if you eat a lot.

Elephant-Ear Fern

An elephant
Is a ruminant
Who can dunk his trunk
In a lake for a drink.
If he wants it hot, there's the kitchen sink.
If he wants it cold, there's a skating rink.

A fernlike plant
In a restaurant
(Chinese) I hear
Is the elephant-ear.
It's served in dishes that are nice and gooey
Like chicken chow mein and plain chop suey.

Snakebark

"It didn't do much for snakes, the Garden—
Not Madison Square, you fool—It's Eden
I'm talking about. A cautionary
Tale at best to scare the wary;
I'd rather be a snake in the grass
With a bit of style, a touch of class,
Than your average Mr. Ordinary."

The Snakebark tree is horrid—horrider
Even than its native state: Florida.

Catnip and Dogwood

A cat's quite different from a dog
And you name it differently, too;
A library cat might be Catalogue,
And a Siamese, Fu Manchu.
Dogs usually have humdrum names
Like Molly, Blacky, Biff, and James.

Cats eat catnip excitedly,
Get drunk and jump around,
But a dog can sniff at a dogwood tree,
And sniff and sniff quite diligently,
Sit down and never budge—
And be as smug and sober as a judge.

Monkey Puzzle Tree

Could a monkey puzzle
Possibly be
A crossword puzzle
Kind of monkey tree?

Does it have leafy
Sorts of crossed sticks
As puzzling, perhaps,
As double acrostics?

Or is it built
On a simpler plan,
Straight up and down
Like an anagram?

Or is it a twisted,
Knotted thing,
Like a cat's cradle
Made of string?

I think that I shall never see
A monkey in a monkey puzzle tree.

Tiger Lily

The tiger does not think the lion is
The king of beasts because the tiger is.
To prove the point, the tiger says,
"I've *fearful* stripes. And he's opaque.
I've symmetry. See William Blake."

The tiger lily doesn't think at all.
It springs up in the spring. And falls in the fall.

Sweet William and Black-Eyed Susan

Since man is a kind of animal, too,
We'll put a boy and girl inside our zoo:

Sweet William's nerves are never overwrought,
And Black-Eyed Susan calls him Bill for short.